Purple Ronnie's Guide to Men

Also by Purple Ronnie

Purple Ronnie's Book of Love

☆

Purple Ronnie's Guide to Life

☆

The Smashing World of Purple Ronnie

☆

Purple Ronnie's Star Signs

☆

Purple Ronnie's Love Poems

☆

The Very Best of Purple Ronnie

Published in 1996 by Statics (London) Ltd,
41 Standard Road, London NW10 6HF
Tel: 0181 965 3327

©1996 Purple Enterprises Ltd.

ISBN 1-873922-53-1

Print Origination by Diva Graphics

Printed in England by H.P.H. Print Ltd.
Unit 3, Royal London Estate, 29 North Acton Road
London NW10 6PE

Words by: Giles Andreae
Pictures by: Janet Cronin and Giles Andreae

Contents

 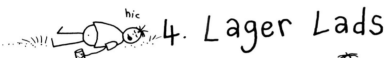

THIS BOOK IS DEDICATED
TO ALL MY FRIENDS
AROUND THE WORLD

a poem about ↓

Arty Men

Arty Men like to be different
To show how creative they are
So don't be surprised
If they butter their thighs
And start barking out loud at your car

How to Spot an Arty Man

Body

Arty Men have long floaty hair to make themselves look dreamy and mysterious

They also like to experiment with growing strange beards and moustaches

Clothes

Arty Men wear the kind of clothes no other man would wear in a million years

What are Arty Men Like?

Character

An Arty Man's brain is on a completely different planet to everyone else's brains

This can mean that they don't always do things you expect

Arty Men are always trying out new ways of muddling up their heads

Sense of Humour
Arty Men have quite a cruel sense of humour

What Do Arty Men Do?

Work

Arty Men are too busy getting in touch with their inner selves to do any proper work

Hobbies

Arty Men are very keen on making things out of stuff they find lying around

Interests

Arty Men love the birds, the bees, the flowers and the trees

Arty Men and Romance

Arty Men are incredibly romantic and they know exactly how to make you feel special

Warning:- Arty Men love to wake you up to watch the sunrise

When it comes to DoingIt, no-one is more creative than an Arty Man

Special Tip:-

Arty Men like to Do It with lots of people all at the same time

a poem about Macho Men

Some men think it's cool to bare
A bulging chest with loads of hair
But if you talk to one you'll find
His brains are stuck up his behind

How to Spot a Macho Man

Body.

Macho Men's bodies are covered with ginormous rippling muscles which they like to oil so they look even bigger

Macho Men's muscles work so well that they can even open beer bottles with their bottoms

Sometimes it can be difficult to find a Macho Man's doodah because there are so many muscles in the way

Clothes

Macho Men mostly think that clothes are for girls but they like to wear teeny outfits that show off their bodies

What are Macho Men Like?

Character

Macho Men's heads are full of dried up mashed potato

This means that Macho Men can be quite difficult to talk to

Sense of Humour

Macho Men are not very good at remembering jokes with words in them

Macho Men don't really understand jokes anyway

What Do Macho Men Do?

Work

Macho Men are born to hang out in the gym so most of them are fitness instructors or sports coaches

Hobbies

Macho Men love looking cool on ginormous motorbikes

Interests

What Macho Men like doing best is gazing at their bodies in gigantic mirrors

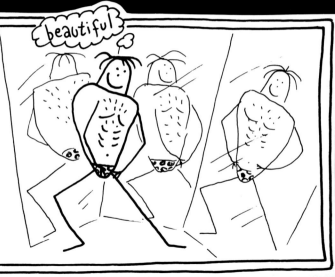

Macho Men and Romance

When it comes to chatting up, some girls think Macho Men are so gorgeous that it doesn't matter what they say

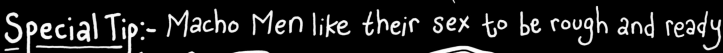

Special Tip:- Macho Men like their sex to be rough and ready

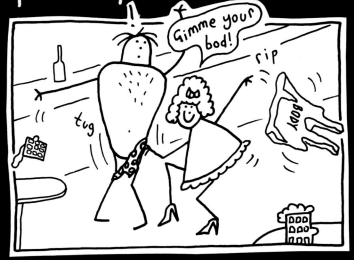

Macho Men love shouting and screaming and often they think they are making love with themselves

Warning:- Do not expect a Macho Man to cuddle you after Doing It

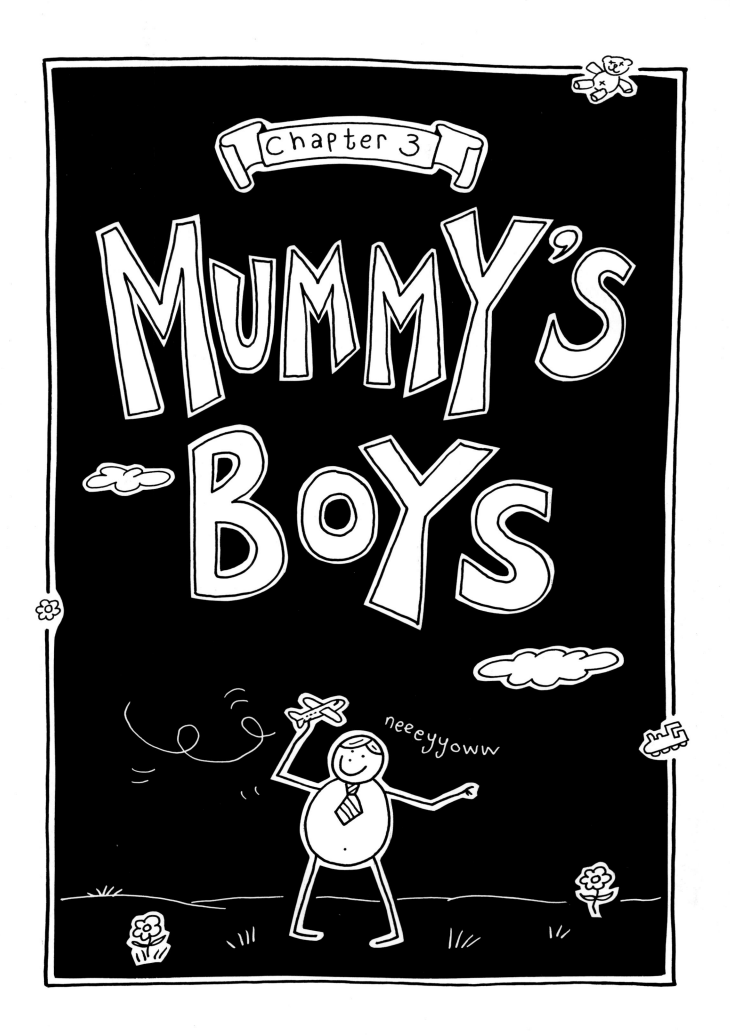

a poem about ↓ Mummy's Boys

When you date a Mummy's Boy
They always bring their Mums
Then sit there cuddling their shawls
And sucking on their thumbs

How to Spot a Mummy's Boy

Body

Mummy's Boys have big fat tummies and chubby cheeks because their Mums have always thought they needed feeding up

They also have soft pasty skins because they have been scrubbed, polished and powdered so often

Mummy's Boys <u>always</u> brush their hair

Clothes

Mummy's Boys' clothes are incredibly clean

...they have creases in everything

and they always smell of roses

What are Mummy's Boys Like?

Character

Mummy's Boys have always been told how great they are so it is best not to disagree with them

A Mummy's Boy is not very good at making decisions on his own

Sense of Humour

Mummy's Boys love making jokes about other people

but it is best not to make jokes about a Mummy's Boy

What Do Mummy's Boys Do?

Work

Mummy's Boys don't really understand about jobs and they never seem to keep them for very long

Hobbies

There's nothing a Mummy's Boy loves more than collecting things

Interests

What Mummy's Boys like most of all is a good story at bath time

Mummy's Boys and Romance

If you go on a date with a Mummy's Boy it is not always very romantic

Mummy's Boys love dressing up in nappies and going to saucy clubs

Special Tip:-
A Mummy's Boy loves nothing better than a good spanking

Warning:-
There is only one person a Mummy's Boy really loves

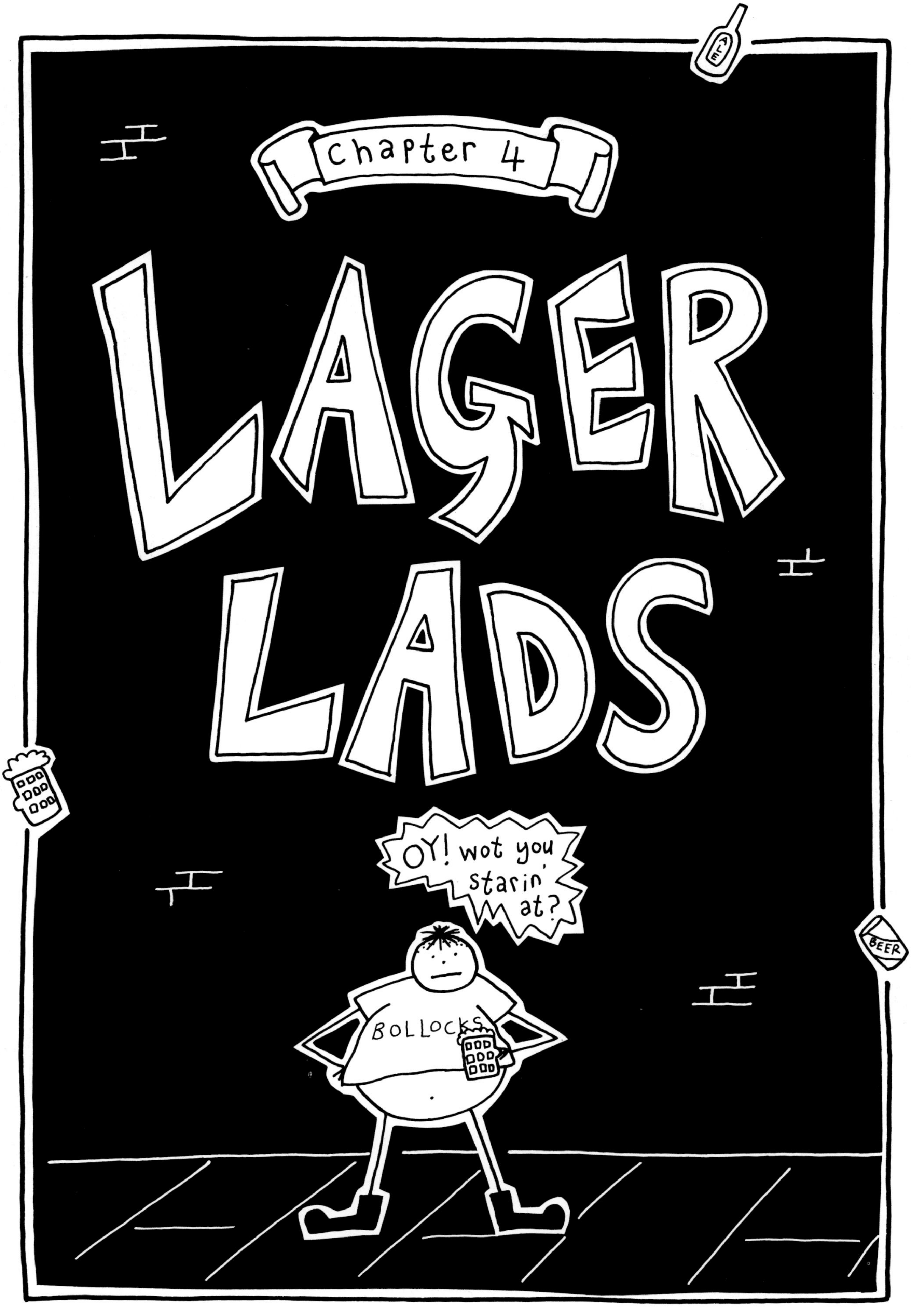

Chapter 4
LAGER LADS
OY! wot you starin' at?
BOLLOCKS
ALE
BEER

a poem about Lager Lads

Lager Lads love going out with their mates

In fact it's their favourite trick

To gobble down masses of curry and beer

And pass out in piles of sick

How to Spot a Lager Lad

Body

Lager Lads have hairy backs and big strong arms which they get from lifting millions of pints of beer

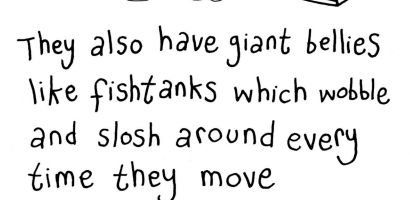

They also have giant bellies like fishtanks which wobble and slosh around every time they move

Clothes

Lager Lads like to wear T-Shirts with their favourite expressions on so they don't need to stop drinking in order to talk

When Lager Lads go on holiday they wear flags on their pants so the police can tell where they come from

What are Lager Lads Like?

Character

Lager Lads love getting together with their mates for an interesting chat

but they are not much good if you want to talk to them on their own

Sense of Humour

A Lager Lad's favourite joke is showing his bottom to people

They also love playing funny tricks on their friends

What Do Lager Lads Do?

Work

Lager Lads dream about being professional sportsmen

Hobbies

A Lager Lad's favourite hobby is picking fights and nutting people

Interests

Lager Lads love nothing better than singing their favourite tunes

Lager Lads and Romance

Warning:-
If you go on a date with a Lager Lad it is best to choose where to go yourself

Lager Lads fall in love with girls who can drink them under the table

Lager Lads have their own special way of telling you they love you

Special Tip:- Sometimes you have to be very patient if you want to Do It with a Lager Lad

Chapter 5

WEEDS

....um

a poem about ↓ Weeds

Some Men think weeds are pathetic
Because they're so fussy and neat
 But most people find
That they're friendly and kind
And girls always say that they're sweet

How to Spot a Weed

Body

Sometimes it is difficult to spot a weed because they are so skinny that you can't always see them from sideways on

When weeds become grown-ups they get two straggly hairs on their chests which they are very proud of

this is Eric and this is Ian

But they still don't need to shave till they are grandads

false beard

tug

Clothes

Weeds try to find clothes that make them look hunky

Yeah!

secret shoulder pads

But even wetsuits look baggy on weeds

shiver

What are Weeds Like?

Character

Weeds are usually very clever. They love reading and filling their brains with all sorts of new ideas

But weeds are not boring. Most weeds have a cool and groovy streak in them

Sense of Humour

Weeds have a great sense of humour and they even like telling jokes about themselves

What Do Weeds Do?

Work

Weeds often work as teachers because bossing people around makes them feel important

Hobbies

Weeds like playing indoor games because outdoor ones are too rough

Interests

Weeds love to go for a little swim to help build up their muscles

Weeds and Romance

Weeds love getting everything ready for romance but they are sometimes quite shy about making a move

Warning:-

Weeds are worried about the size of their bits so they don't like Doing It with the lights on

Weeds always ask before they do anything

and they are always very polite afterwards

Special Tip:-

Weeds like to keep their privates clean and tidy

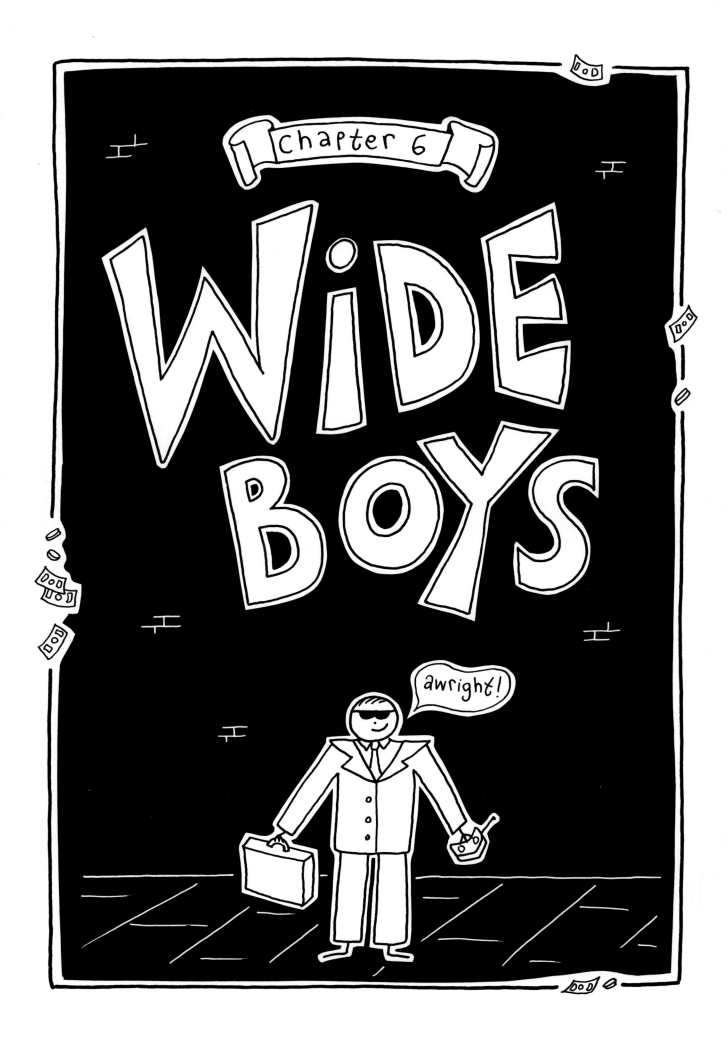

a poem about Wide Boys

They're always on their mobile phones
cutting dodgy deals
Looking sharp in shiny suits
And nifty sets of wheels

How to Spot a Wide Boy

Body

Most Wide Boys look after their bodies because they think that looking good is the most important thing in the world

Wide Boys only have 2 hairstyles:—

1. the slicked-back wet look

2. the stupid perm

Clothes

Every good Wide Boy wears a sharp suit with shades

Wide Boys like to be seen in very smart pants

What are Wide Boys Like?

Character

Wide Boys are incredibly friendly to everyone cos they never know when they might need a favour

Wide Boys are very good at keeping in touch because they love to use their mobile phones

Sense of Humour

There's nothing a Wide Boy likes more than telling a really filthy joke

Work

The only job Wide Boys ever do is selling things. Wide Boys can sell _anything_

Hobbies

Wide Boys are always keen to show off their latest toys

Interests

Wide Boys love to have a saucy night out on the town with their mates

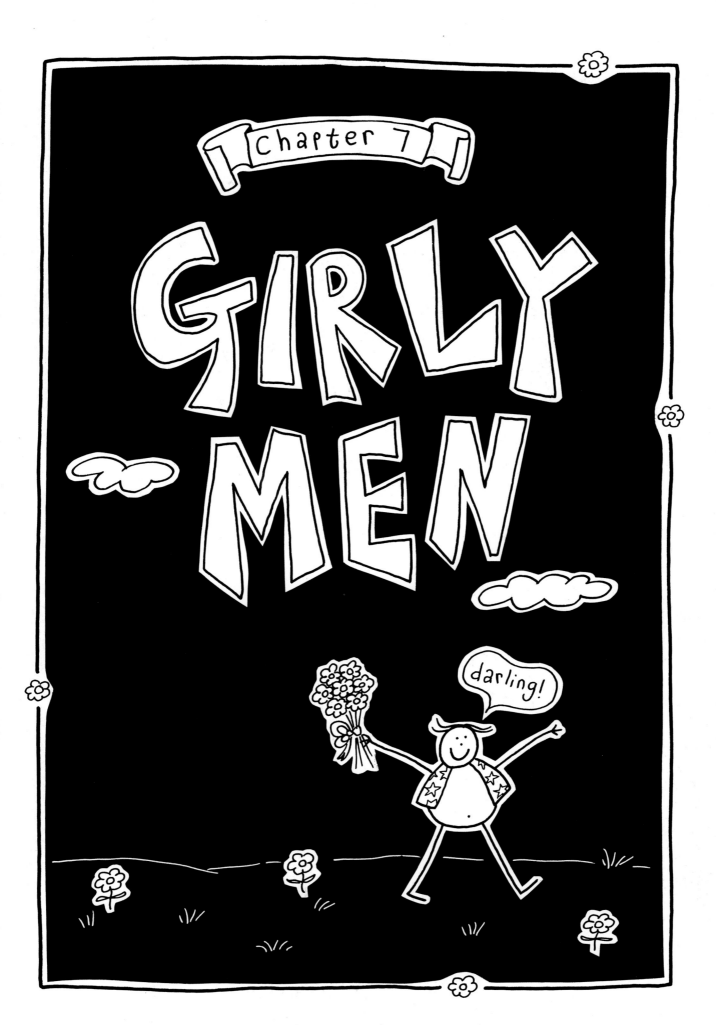

a poem about
Girly Men

Girly Men think playing sport is too rough

So they love to go shopping instead

And when they get home

They spend hours on the phone

Before wearing their face masks to bed

gossip, natter, chat, giggle

How to Spot a Girly Man

Body

No-one pampers their body quite like a Girly Man does

Girly Men's bathrooms are stuffed full of all sorts of lotions and potions for making themselves feel gorgeous

Clothes

A Girly Man has masses of expensive clothes with other people's names written on them

Girly Men spend even longer getting dressed than girls do

What Are Girly Men Like?

Character

Girly Men could easily spend their whole lives nattering

But they are never any good at making important decisions

Girly Men dream of a world where you don't ever have to get your hands dirty

Sense of Humour

Girly Men love gossiping and telling naughty stories about their friends

What Do Girly Men Do?

Work

Girly Men are completely mad about fashion, the arts and design

Hobbies

A Girly Man likes to go on sunny holidays to get all brown and handsome

Interests

There is nothing a Girly Man loves more than shopping

Girly Men and Romance

Girly Men are very tender and sensual and they <u>love</u> touching and stroking

Girly Men often prefer reading mags and chatting to actually Doing It

<u>Warning</u>:- Do not be surprised if a Girly Man wants to put on your undies

<u>Special Tip</u>:- If you are Doing It with a Girly Man you must be careful not to mess up his hairstyle or you will put him off completely

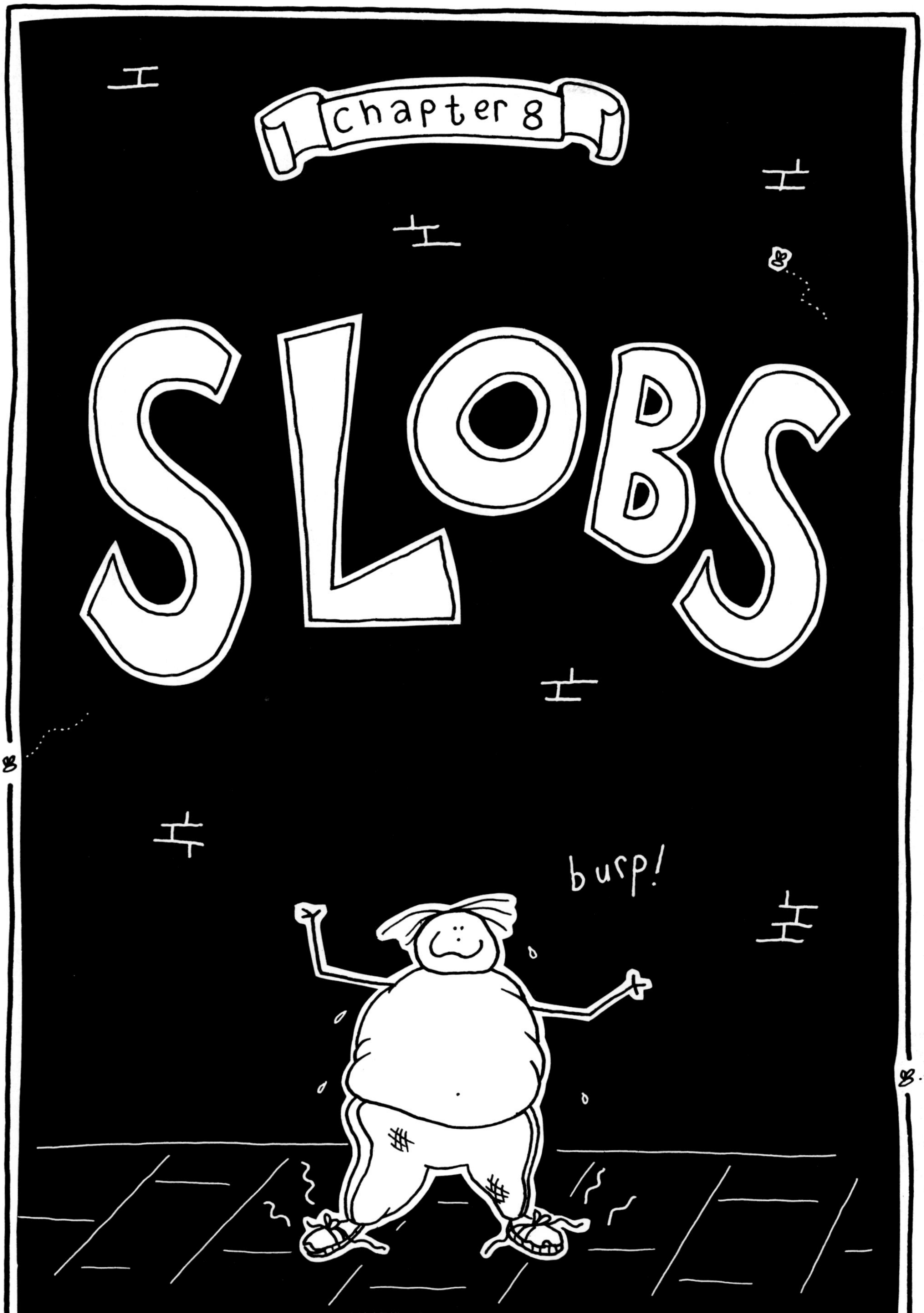
chapter 8
SLOBS
burp!

a poem about Slobs

They walk around in clouds of smoke
They splutter burp and wheeze
They live off mouldy sausages
And whiff of rancid cheese

How to Spot a Slob

Body

A Slob's body is made up of huge rolls of lard which are separated by white sweaty creases

You always know when a slob is nearby because you can smell them coming before you even see them

Clothes

Slobs wear whatever's on the floor when they get up in the morning

A Slob has one pair of trainers which he wears all the time because they are glued to his feet with toe cheese

What are Slobs Like?

Character

A Slob is a brilliant person to tell your secrets to because he can't ever be bothered to talk and he only likes to use his brain to remember important information

Slobs are just as happy on their own...

...as they are with other people

Sense of Humour

Slobs love nothing better than going to the gym for a good giggle at the exercise classes

What Do Slobs Do?

Work

If slobs have to work they like to do something they find interesting

Hobbies

Slobs are very good at Quiz shows

Interests

A Slob likes to keep in touch with all the latest bits of technology

Slobs and Romance

A Slob's favourite kind of date is to have a cosy dinner for two at home

Slobs love giving their girlfriends chocolates but it is always best to keep them in a safe place

Special Tips:-

1. Slobs usually prefer <u>watching</u> rude vids to <u>doing</u> rude things

2. There is only one position that Slobs ever like Doing It in

SPORT MEN

goal!

a poem about a
Sport Man

No girl can get close to a Sport Man
Without passing out on the spot
The air in his room
Has the subtle perfume
Of the sweat on a wrestler's bot

How to Spot a Sport Man

Body
Sport Men spend their whole time getting every little bit of their bodies into shape

Some of them shave parts of their bodies to make themselves go even faster

Clothes
Sport Men *love* their kit and they cannot resist wearing it everywhere they go

What are Sport Men Like?

Character

Sport Man is incredibly competitive and always needs to be the best at everything

Sport Men love to have stimulating conversations with their mates

Sense of Humour

Sport Men spend many happy hours laughing at each other's parts in the shower

What Do Sport Men Do?

Work

Sport Men love to work in shops where they can get their hands on all the latest gear

Hobbies

Sport Men have a habit of commentating on everything they do

Interests

Sport Men like nothing better than spending the whole weekend shouting at the T.V.

Sport Men and Romance

A Sport Man loves to take his girlfriend off on romantic holidays

Special Tip:- If you want to really turn a Sport Man on it is best to wear his team's home strip when you go to bed

<u>Warning</u>:- Sport Men like to Do It in very athletic positions

Sport Men always time their performance in bed

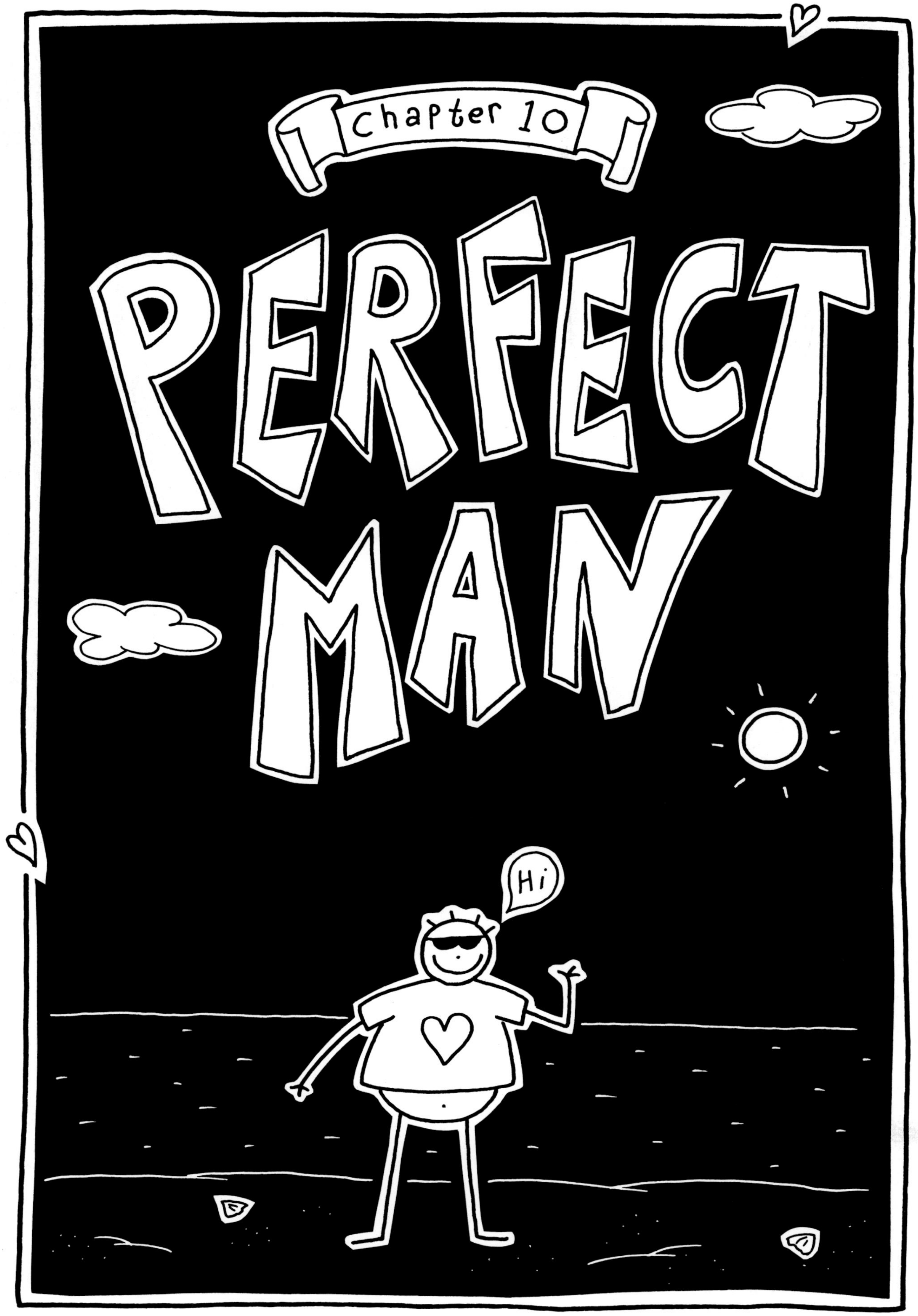

Chapter 10
PERFECT MAN
Hi

a poem about a ↓ Perfect Man

Most girls want a man who is perfect
But maybe not many exist
Who've got charm and panache
Several sackloads of cash
And a willy the size of your wrist

How to Spot a Perfect Man

Body

A Perfect Man's body would win any competition even though he would never dream of entering one

The Perfect Man has a gorgeous smile that lights up in his eyes every time he sees you

Clothes:-

Perfect Men are not half as interested in buying clothes for themselves as they are in buying clothes for you

Perfect Men never complain when you borrow their clothes

What Do Perfect Men Do?

Work

Perfect Men love working so they can make lots of money and take you on smashing holidays

Hobbies

A Perfect Man's favourite hobby is cooking

Interests

Perfect Men are only ever interested in you

Perfect Men and Romance

The Perfect Man loves to tell you how beautiful you look - even first thing in the morning

Perfect Men always find a reason to take you out for a romantic evening

When it comes to Doing It :-

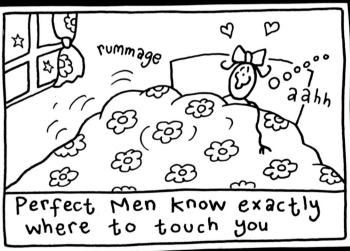

Perfect Men know exactly where to touch you

and they can keep going all night long

Special Tip:-
Perfect Men always cuddle you until you fall asleep